The best stories are simple
as originally developed by the indige...
ethnologists as "The Straits Salish" and as practiced exclusively in
today's Salish Sea in northwest Washington State is one of those
"best stories."

This book is not an attempt to create a definitive "history" of the reef
net fishery; that is something to be saved for an enterprising
historian of the future.

This book *is* an attempt to tell the story of one of the most unique,
and interesting methods of catching salmon ever developed; the reef
net as invented by an unknown genius among the Straits Salish

peoples of hundreds of years ago.
This book is also an attempt to
examine the lessons to be learned
from the past and their potential for
informing the future; what can we
learn from the past to enhance our
approach to the future?

The lessons of the reef net include
respect for a people capable of
developing an advanced technology
based on the natural world they lived
in. The lessons of the reef net lead to
an increased respect for the
environment. The lessons of the reef net include material for
reflection about the value of self-reliance and an entrepreneurial
spirit. The lessons of the reef net have much to teach about the
value of community and people working in a common cause.

We hope you enjoy this effort and we value any thoughts you might,
as a reader, want to pass on to us. Don't be surprised to find your
suggestions adopted into future editions of this book.

Mark Shintaffer

Jack Petree

Reef Nets

The Original Environmentally Sensitive Technology

"The term, selective fishing, has been used to describe any of several fishing gears and management objectives, **yet at its most basic definition a selective fishery is one in which by catch** (the capture of undesired species) **is avoided altogether or is able to be released alive and unharmed.**

As the Department of Fish & Wildlife has experimented with selective commercial fishing gear and moved toward selective fishing practices in recreational fishing, **reef nets stand out as the original and still the best in selective fishing.**

Practiced by the Indians of the Puget Sound region using materials gathered locally, reef nets are unique to the area. Modern materials and hydraulics have improved efficiency but the basic methods remain the same. Reef nets do not gill or surround salmon with a net. Rather they count on natural and manmade structures to lead the salmon into a shallow laid net which is then lifted and the fish spilled into holding pens.

Minimal handling and stress coupled with the ability to keep the fish alive make reef nets the most selective fishing gear available. Reef nets are fixed to one location and only catch migrating adult salmon that swim through their gear. For years reef nets have released non-target salmon species when management needs dictate. Mortality and bycatch are lower than any other fishing gear. Today reef nets are used in northern Puget Sound, targeting sockeye and pink salmon during summer months and coho and chum salmon during the fall."

From the Washington Department of Fish and Wildlife website:

(Bolds added)

http://wdfw.wa.gov/fishing/commercial/salmon/reef_nets.html

2

The Pre-Contact Reef Net Fishery In American Waters

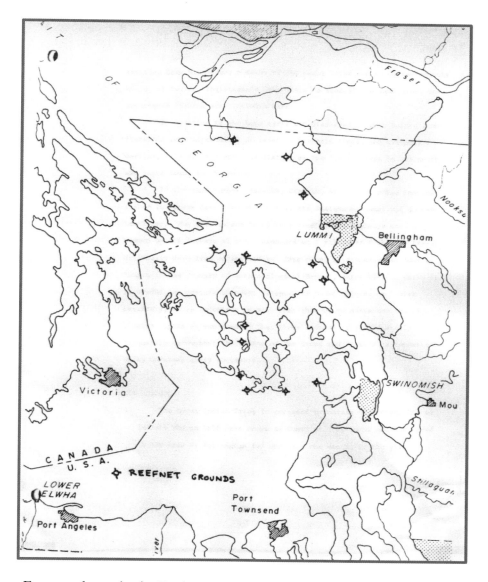

From anthropologist Barbara Lane's testimony in the Boldt Fishing
Rights Case – 1973
(Some additional sites have been identified by other anthropologists)

The Origin Of Salish Reef Nets – Lost In The Mist Of Time

Richard Rathbun, one of the United State's most renowned fisheries experts in the late 1800s described conditions existing in the early days of the settlement of the region surrounding today's San Juan Islands. According to Rathbun:

The Indians were fishing in this region when it was first invaded by the whites. They were, then, however, solely concerned in supplying their own domestic wants, using apparently the same appliances they do to-day, reef nets and hooks and lines in the salt water, and spears, dip nets, and weirs in the rivers. Traders reached the upper Fraser early in the century (1800s) thence working to the sea, and the salmon became one of their most important foods, being obtained partly by their own efforts and partly of the Indians. The latter gradually developed into commercial fishermen, and to-day (1900) constitute a prominent element in the fishing fraternity.

No one knows who invented the reef net system as used by speakers of the Straits Salish language in the early days of settlement. Some have speculated a Hudsons Bay employee or a missionary taught the indigenous peoples the technique; speculation that seems unlikely for a number of reasons. Most early anthropologists rejected or simply did not address the notion though anthropologist Barbara Lane provides convincing circumstantial evidence the technology was devised by indigenous peoples well before contact.

More recent work examining reef net locations using modern diving equipment should put an end to any such speculation; anthropologist N. Alexander Easton, in the 1980s and '90s examined known indigenous reef net sites in Canada and physically counted the large stones used as anchors by the indigenous peoples (anchor stones could not be raised once dropped in place, it took several men to lift them onto the boats for transport to the net location so new stones had to be sunk every year). Easton's estimates indicate most sites came to be utilized sometime between the 1400s and the 1600s, long before either the Hudson's Bay Company or missionaries were active in the area.

Still, no one actually does know when the reef net technology was first invented, where it was first put to use, or how an early innovator, or innovators, came to the realization that setting up a net between two canoes in a way that imitated a natural reef located in the path of one of the world's great fish runs could allow many more sockeye salmon to be caught, many times more efficiently and, with less damage to the fish than had ever been possible before.

What *is* known is that the reef nets developed and utilized by the indigenous peoples living along the shores of today's Straits of Georgia, the San Juan Islands, parts of Whatcom County, Washington and near the mouth of Washington's Skagit River (another argument against the idea that an outsider would have had the specific knowledge about the structure of the region's sea bottom as well as the habits of the Fraser River sockeye necessary to "invent" an entirely new technology specific to the capture of that particular fish) profoundly changed the economy, the social structures, and the quality of life of those inhabiting the shores of parts of the inland "sea" prior to first contact with the Europeans.

To the indigenous peoples of the region the specialized knowledge and the special nature of the fish reef nets were especially utilized to capture meant wealth for the owners of a reef net location. The accumulation of wealth was an important focus of Northwest native culture; wealth was considered evidence of special favor granted the holder of the wealth, favor giving the holder honor, prestige, and exalted position in the social structure of the community.

Barbara Lane, one of the most renowned of anthropologists investigating the lives of the indigenous peoples before contact with, primarily, European explorers spoke to the special benefits the reef net fishery provided those able to use the technology. Writing about the forbearers of today's Lummi tribe Lane wrote, in the 1970s, *"While fishing was central to the basic economy of all Indians in western Washington, the Lummi...had access to unusually productive fisheries. The abundance and variety of marine resources, coupled with a highly specialized technology for harvesting permitted a high standard of living as well as surpluses to trade for imported commodities."*

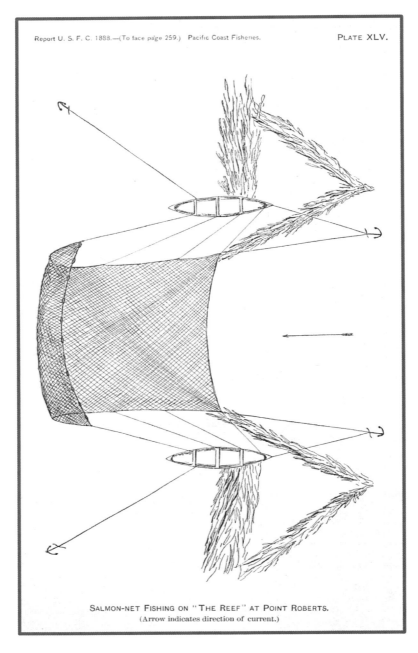

SALMON-NET FISHING ON "THE REEF" AT POINT ROBERTS.
(Arrow indicates direction of current.)

Illustration of indigenous reef net set up from 1888
Report On The Fisheries of the Pacific Coast Of the United States

A Native American Leonardo

The inventor/inventors of the technology we know today as reef net fishing, had to have had a bit of Leonardo da Vinci-like genius. Only the same kind of "thinking outside the box" that Leonardo exhibited would have resulted in the complex, yet simple, technology involved in reef netting.

The indigenous man (probably a man given the structure of the culture of the day) who first devised the reef net is, in one way, a step up on Leonardo; the reef net technology first used those unknown years ago was more than a flash of inspiration in someone's mind. Unlike Leonardo's speculations, the basic construction of the tool devised all those years ago has come down, with minor modification, to us today. Leonardo's ideas and concepts were just that, suggestions of what could be in some unknown future. The reef net, on the other hand, fed hungry people the day it was invented, provided an economic boost to those using the technology, and, in modern times, the reef net continues to provide the fish that has meant so much to so many for so long.

Indians Reef Netting for Salmon at Lummi Isl.—June 1898—BertHunton Photo

The People Of The Reef Net – The Straits Salish

With only a few exceptions, the indigenous peoples who were living south of the northern portions of Canada's Gulf of Georgia, north of about Tillamook, Oregon, and west of the Cascade range of mountains in pre-contact times are, because of some linguistic and cultural similarities, referred to as the Coast Salish. That does not mean, however, that all of the peoples of the area were alike, or even very much alike, culturally. Nor does it mean that a common language prevailed throughout the region. According to anthropologists studying the pre-contact lives of peoples of the area, even very close neighbors would have had linguistic differences with cultural differences evident even from village to village.

In fact, much of what is, in the everyday world of casual discussion, generally assumed to be true about the indigenous peoples inhabiting the shorelines and utilizing the waters of Southern British Columbia, Canada, the Straits of Juan de Fuca, and Northwest Washington's Puget Sound before treaty times is, at best, inaccurate and, at worst, fantasy.

First, most casual discussion today assumes the "tribes" of the region were pretty much indistinguishable from one another or, at least very similar one to another. That assumption is like characterizing the Celts, Vandals, Huns, Danes, Anglos, Picts, Gaul's, and other tribes of Europe as being part and parcel of a single civilization. In fact, the modern day concept of "tribes" is an artifice imposed on the indigenous peoples of the West Coast of North America by the treaty makers of the 1800s. Anthropologists have generally agreed the very concept of "tribe," as we defined the term today would have been foreign to the indigenous peoples living along the coastlines of today's Washington State and British Columbia.

Within the context of the overall description of the Coast Salish as a grouping of indigenous peoples, the Straits Salish were a people apart. As described by Wayne Prescott Suttles (Generally recognized as the dean of anthropologists focusing on the indigenous peoples living in what is now the Northwest region of the United States and Southwestern, British Columbia, Canada), the Straits

Salish can be defined as the peoples who *"...shared a common language; and they shared a common pattern in their relationship to their habitat, a greater adaptation to life on salt-water channels than that of their Salish neighbors, with an emphasis upon reef-netting for sock-eye salmon in the channels."*

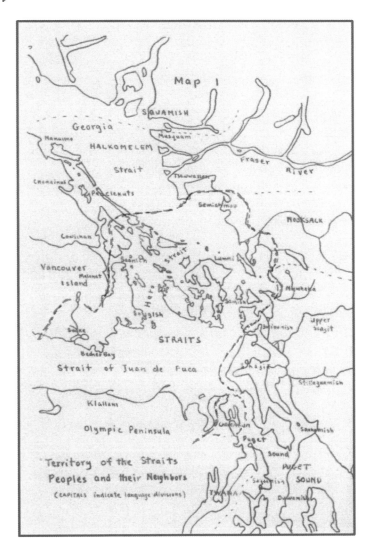

From: Wayne Prescott Suttles – *Economic Life Of The Coast Salish Of Haro And Rosario Straits* Expert witness before the Indian Claims Commission (Color added for better understanding)

Though a people apart, distinct from other Salish peoples as described by Suttles, the peoples of today's inland sea, (now formally described as "The Salish Sea" by the geographical authorities of both Canada and the United States) did have, in pre-contact times, much in common with their Coast Salish neighbors as well; there was no defined "tribal" identity, the idea of "chiefs," as the term is commonly understood today, did not exist, and in many cases some would have struggled to understand the speech used in even nearby villages.

As explained by Carroll Riley, an ethnologist also providing expert witness testimony to the Indian Claims Commission on behalf of the tribes in the 1950s and '60s, some significant commonalities among the Coast Salish peoples in general included:

1. *"The largest close-knit unit in western Washington society was the village.*

2. *Political authority was on the village level and was very weak. The leaders were those who, by reason of birth and wealth, had prestige in the community.*

3. *The land-using unit was the village. This group made intensive use of fishing, hunting, and gathering lands in the vicinity of the actual settlement. Other territory was used sporadically in hunting and collecting.*

4. *Access to village territory was available to outsiders. There was a feeling, however, on the part of both host and visitor that such territory belonged to the home group."*

As Suttles pointed out, the Straits Salish's use of reef nets set them apart as that net's use was intimately tied to one of the world's great fish runs; the sockeye salmon rush to the Fraser and Skagit Rivers. Despite the huge size of the runs, sockeye were certainly only available, in pre-contact days, in limited quantities outside of the river systems leading to inland spawning grounds; until the reef net!

The Significance Of Sockeye And Of The Reef Net To The People Of The Straits Salish

Suttles lists the "tribes" of the Straits Salish as being today's Sooke, Songish, and Saanich in British Columbia, and the Semiahmoo, Lummi, and Samish of Washington. All six groups spoke a language somewhat understandable by the others but generally incomprehensible to the peoples both to the north and to the south . All utilized the reef net, a technology not used by tribes to either the north or south. In common with all the shore dwelling indigenous peoples of the northwest, the religious, social, and political lives of the indigenous inhabitants centered on fish but, to the Straits Salish, inhabiting the inland sea south of the Fraser River and east of the Straits of Juan de Fuca, the sockeye was king!

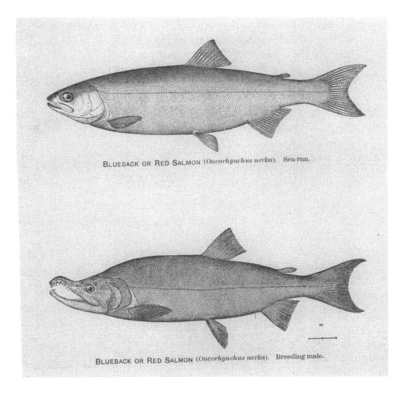

BLUEBACK OR RED SALMON (*Oncorhynchus nerka*). Sea-run.

BLUEBACK OR RED SALMON (*Oncorhynchus nerka*). Breeding male.

John Cobb *Salmon Fisheries of the Pacific Coast* ca. 1910

"Unusually Productive Fisheries"

Sockeye salmon were the reason anthropologist Lane wrote about the "…unusually productive fisheries" when she studied the life and culture of today's Lummi. The "…highly specialized technology for harvesting…" Lane pointed to was the reef net.

For the indigenous fisherman the sockeye was exceptionally prized both for its taste and for its nutritious flesh. However, for those same indigenous peoples living along the shores of Washington and southern British Columbia's inland sea, sockeye were almost certainly, in the pre-reef net days, a scarce commodity.

The unusual nature of the fish accounts for that scarcity.

Among the Pacific salmon, sockeye are the only species that feeds almost exclusively on plankton for most of their lives at sea so they are not typically drawn to lures, especially as they make the run from the ocean to their birth lakes and streams. An indigenous fisherman, using available technology, whether fishing with a line, a spear, or an ordinary net would have found it difficult to catch more than the occasional sea run Sockeye.

River fishing in what we now call the Salish Sea would also have been unavailable to most of the inhabitants of the former Puget Sound and the northern regions of the Georgia Straits. Only the great Fraser river and, to a limited extent, the Skagit River housed sockeye runs of any size.

The lack of sockeye in the rest of the river systems of the region comes from the fact that sockeye, save for the occasional stray, do not ascend rivers without lakes. For the most part sockeye juveniles require a lake environment for the first two or three years of their lives. In all of Puget Sound only the Skagit River provides significant and suitable sockeye habitat due to the existence of Baker Lake. In pre-contact days a small population of sockeye is said to have also made the run into Lake Washington but it, by all accounts, was an insignificant population. Lake Washington's Sockeye of today are reportedly entirely the descendants of fish transplanted from Baker Lake after the locks connecting the sound with Lake Washington were built and any natural run was cut off from the lake by the elimination of the Black River and a nine foot drop in the water level in the lake as a result of the building project.

As the sockeye approaches the rivers leading to its spawning grounds it begins to transform. The fish arriving at those grounds is a different kind of fish than the mighty swimmer first entering the waters of the Salish Sea. As the male Sockeye, especially, closes on its target river it begins to change shape, color, and, its flesh changes in consistency. The head elongates, developing a distinctive hooked snout and obvious teeth; the heads turn green and the body takes on a distinctive red coloration. Females also change color though the changes to their head shape are less noticeable.

To many, the river version of the fish is an inferior fish in terms of both taste and of the consistency of the flesh compared to the sea run creature making the sea run sockeye an especially valuable commodity, today and in the ancient past.

The unique characteristics of the sea run Sockeye all combined, in pre-contact times, to create a resource that was "pink gold" for the indigenous entrepreneur able to exploit the resource.

Reef Netting In Pioneer Times

When pioneers from the east began to arrive in the Puget Sound region, the indigenous peoples of the area were the acknowledged experts when it came to exploiting the marine resources of the sound and the straits. From the earliest days trappers, traders, settlers, and others pouring into the northwest depended on the Indians to supply them with fish. In the regions of the Sound where the Sockeye ran a few intrepid entrepreneurs gave reef nets a try but, for the most part, they were unsuccessful, lacking both the knowledge of the Sound necessary to place the nets, and the skill needed to operate a reef net set effectively; a skill finely honed over hundreds of years by the Straits Salish. Pioneer fishermen simply couldn't compete.

An early description of the Indian reef net was provided by Assistant Secretary of the Smithsonian, Richard Rathbun, in 1895. As described by Rathbun:

"The reef net is the exclusive property of the Indians, by whom it has long been used. Its name is derived from the character of sea bottom for which it is specially adapted—the peculiar kelp covered reefs—but while such abound throughout the region, the number over which the sockeye pass in sufficient quantity to furnish good fishing seems to be comparatively small.

Formerly the nets were made from the fiber of cedar bark or' roots, the preparation of which was a winter occupation and consumed much time. Cotton twine is now used and since its introduction the nets have been enlarged. They consist of a piece of webbing, which varies more or less in size, but may average perhaps from 36 to 40 feet long by 25 to 30 feet across, the mesh being about 3 ½ inches.

To prepare for fishing a channel of suitable width is cut through the kelp, and in this the net is set between two canoes so anchored from both ends as to keep them parallel with and at the sides of the passageway.

The suspension of the net is accomplished by means of guy lines leading from the canoes and head anchors. In the position which it then assumes the front end, facing the current, sinks near the bottom, while the hind end curves to near the surface. Although the kelp may be quite submerged along the sides of the channel, still it tends to direct the fish toward the net, and their movements may still further be controlled by short leads of kelp run out from the front corners of the latter. In case the depth of water is too great, ropes are sometimes stretched across the channel below the front margin of the net, and to these bunches of reeds may be attached with the object of turning the fish upward.

The salmon, approaching with the current, pass upon the net. They do not mesh, nor is there anything to prevent their escaping at the sides. It is at this point that the Indians are required to display their skill An experienced man stands in the bow of each canoe as a lookout, while each of the guy lines is in the hands of a member of the crew.

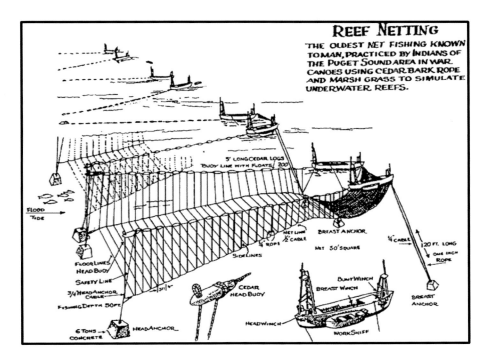

Modern Reef Net depiction from Washington Fish and Wildlife Website

The moment fish are seen coming over the net word is given to haul in, a command which must be promptly obeyed. The side lines leading to the stern anchors are tripped at the same time, causing the boats to come together, so that the net can be gathered up from all sides in a sort of bag. The contents are emptied into the canoes, the net is again thrown over and spread out, and the watching resumed.

Success depends upon the net being hauled quickly and properly at the right moment. Should the fish have turned before the first step is taken, they are likely to escape wholly or in greater part. Constant vigilance is required, but the Indians have become so expert that they seldom fail to land their catch, and their success seems to depend only on the appearance of the fish in sufficient quantity.

When the fish are running well a large reef-net crew will consist of 10 to 15 Indians, as at Point Roberts but in some places the nets are smaller and the crew may not contain more than 6 to 8 men.

On Cannery Point Reef (Point Roberts) *it is said that under exceptionally favorable conditions a haul can be made every 2 or 3 minutes, and a single large catch may fill the two canoes. With fishing at its best a single net may secure as many as 2,000 salmon in a day, but to do this the fishing canoes must continue at their posts, the catch being transferred to shore by other boats.*

The proper time for fishing with these nets is during the set of both the ebb and flood tide, when the current is running not swifter than 5 knots an hour. They can only be used in clear water, as it is essential that the salmon should be plainly seen; when the water is muddy or the surface rough nothing can be done.

While originally the Indians employed this method only for a short period each season to supply their own wants, in recent years they have found a ready sale for their entire catch, which, consisting as it does mainly of sockeye, is in great demand at the canneries. The money value of this species is now so great that they retain only small quantities at the most for drying.

Reef net fishing could not, however, be profitably followed by the whites, owing to the number of hands required to operate the net and the great loss of time resulting from unfavorable conditions of sea and weather. The Indian reef-netters belong partly to the Lummi Reservation and partly to British Columbia. The latter fish chiefly about the San Juan Islands, coming over specially for that purpose."

NOTE: Sockeye also spawned in the Elwha River just east of the present day Port Angeles on Washington's Olympic Peninsula as well as in streams along the open coast of what is now Washington State. The Elwha run is likely to have been quite small. Today's Fish and Wildlife authorities estimate the Elwha river system and its lake could support about 3,000 fish. In addition, sockeye would have run in a direct line from the ocean to the mouth of the Elwha. The anthropological literature seems to contain no references to a reef net fishery near the Olympic Peninsula. What is known is that the Klallam, close relatives to the Straits Salish, sometimes travelled east to fish with the reef netters in and near the San Juan islands.

In a 1921 *Report of the U.S. Commissioner of Fisheries,* John Cobb spoke to the fact that *"As on other bodies of water on the Pacific coast frequented by salmon, the Indians were fishing for them when the first whites visited the country. The natives at this time, and for many years after, used reef nets and hooks and lines in the salt water, and spears, dip nets, and weirs in the rivers."*

Regarding reef nets and their use by the indigenous peoples Cobb reported on "…two of the ancient fisheries on the lower Sound, Point Roberts Reef and Village Point."

According to Cobb, citing to and quoting a work by J. A. Kerr as carried in *Pacific Fisherman* (1917):

"The original reef net of the Indians, as described by the first white settlers and by the Indians themselves, was constructed as follows: The natives peeled the bark from the willow and with it spun a twine and tied a net about 25 feet in width and 40 feet in length, with a mesh substantially of the dimensions and shape of that used in the now familiar pound net.

They then went into the swamps and cut cedar withes. After heating rocks and placing them in pools of water they steamed these withes, after which they twisted them into substantial ropes.

Launching The Canoe – Costello (1895)

Their reef net operations were confined to the shoal waters over the reefs. The reef net locations were of great value to the Indians, and were considered as property and handed down from father to son. As a rule the Indian families controlling these locations owned an inner and outer location. The reef at Point Roberts is over 1 mile in length.

Reef net fishing was confined to the flood tide. At the beginning of the flood the outer location was used, after the middle of the flood the nets were shifted to the inner locations.

The Indians assembled at the reefs in advance of the salmon run and prepared their appliances. They first secured heavy boulders or blocks of sandstone from Chuckanut to be used as anchors. They then procured for each net two logs about the length of their canoes. To each end of these logs they tied one of their ropes, about 100 feet in length, the other end of which was fastened to the stone anchor. These logs were anchored over the top of the reef and about 20 feet apart. From the forward end of these logs there was run out at an angle of 45° other ropes to a distance of 50 feet, the outward end fastened to a buoy. To these ropes were fastened stalks of kelp, the ends weighted to the bottom with stones. Thus was constructed a lead operating to concentrate the approaching school of fish between the logs. Then from the front end of these logs there was dropped forward and to the bottom two ropes, from one of these ropes to the other, at intervals of 2 or 3 feet, were fastened cords of willow twine. This appliance was called by the Indians a ladder.

Now in operating the net itself two canoes were lashed on the inside of the logs. Three Indians occupied one canoe and four the other. The net was then suspended between the canoes. The Indians in the forward end of the canoes held the ropes fastened to the bottom of the net, those in the back end held the ropes fastened to the top of the net. The tide running against the net caused it to bag, or purse. The fourth Indian in one of the canoes was generally an elderly man and was called the watcher. He discovered the school of salmon as they were carried into the net and at his signal the Indians at the front of the canoes pulled the lower edge of the net, which was kept within 4 feet of the surface, above the water. The Indians at the middle of the canoe reached down and caught the sides of the net, lifting the sides above the surface. These Indians pulled against each other, the long ropes by which the logs were moored giving enough to allow the canoes to be pulled alongside each other. The fish were then dumped into one of the canoes, after which the net was loosened and lowered, and the boats fell back to their original position again.

With these appliances the Indians would take up to 3,000 salmon on a single run of the tide. This Indian appliance affords not only an interesting illustration of native ingenuity, but as a matter of fact was the forerunner of the pound net. John Waller, a Welshman, was one of the earliest settlers at Point Roberts. He observed the operations of the reef net and in the early 60's constructed at Point Roberts the first pound net ever driven on the Pacific coast. The leads duplicated that of the Indians, while he impounded the salmon by means of the tunnel leading into a web pot, instead of lifting them as impounded.
The reef net marks the humble Siwash as an inventor of some skill, and as a benefactor of some importance, and the apparatus would be in use to-day were it not for the large number of people required to operate it."

The heart of the cultural, economic, and spiritual influence of the reef net on the peoples of the Straits Salish was the fact that nearly every man, woman, and child was engaged in the fishery while the Sockeye ran. Ethnologist Daniel L. Boxberger estimated that a minimum of 30 reef net gears were operated by the Lummi when the

Treaty of Point Elliot was signed (*The Lummi Island Reef Nets*). Based on a population of about 700, Boxberger concluded, "It is safe to conclude that most, if not all, of the people of the tribe benefitted from the reef net fishery."

NOTE: From treaty times through the first quarter century of the 1900s coastal Indians of the Northwest were commonly called, as a group, the "Siwash." The term comes from the Chinook trade language, a jargon devised to allow communication between indigenous peoples and between indigenous peoples and the settlers, trading companies, and others flooding into the Northwest after treaty times. George Gibbs' 1863 *Dictionary Of The Chinook Jargon, Or, Trade Language Of Oregon* lists the term and identifies it as meaning simply, "Indian."

Today the term "Siwash" is generally considered derogatory and should never be used because of that negative connotation but, in earlier times it was simply a descriptive word in common use by both indigenous peoples and those they communicated with for trade or for other reasons.

Modern Gear Is Not So Different From That Used By The Reef Net's Inventors

Changing Tides

Treaties and other treatments with the Straits Salish and the governments of both the United States and Canada marked a time of immense change for the people of the reef net. Tribes were arbitrarily designated, reservations were delineated, formal governmental organization was installed, and sweeping change in nearly every aspect of the cultural life the indigenous peoples came, in relative terms, almost overnight.

Regarding the economic importance of the reef net fishery, little changed for nearly three decades after the treaty signing. The expertise the Coast Salish had developed over centuries stood them well; their fish was desired by the waves of pioneers seeking out new lands while tribal members wanted the astonishing range of never before seen goods suddenly available in trade for their fish. A thriving economy based on mutual wants and needs came into being. Speaking of the Lummi, Boxberger says tribal fishermen fished "virtually unhindered," until the 1880s and, *"Thus, in a relatively short period the Lummis became enmeshed in the market economy and began to exploit the salmon resources for cash as well as sustenance."*

Then came the crash!

Fish traps were huge devices, some nearly half a mile in length, channeling any fish in the area into a constricted pen where they were removed, shipped to a cannery, and processed. The technique was well developed in the eastern fisheries of the United States and turned out, with some modification, to be especially well suited to exactly the areas reef nets had been developed to exploit.

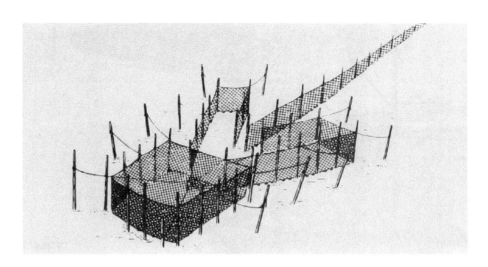

Fish Trap or Pound Net

According to Rathbun, in the land of the Straits Salish, *"Trap-net fishing was started at Point Roberts some years before it was taken up at other places. The first net of this kind was built by John Waller, about 1880, oft' Cannery Point, a short distance north of the Indian reef, and this position appears to have been more continuously occupied for the purpose than any other. For nearly a decade, however, such operations as were carried on were scarcely more than experimental, and the results for the most part were small."*

By the turn of the century, however, traps presented a virtual wall of netting in front of migrating Sockeye. The reef net fishery at Point Roberts was nearly destroyed by the traps while the fishery at Village Point was severely, and negatively, impacted as well.

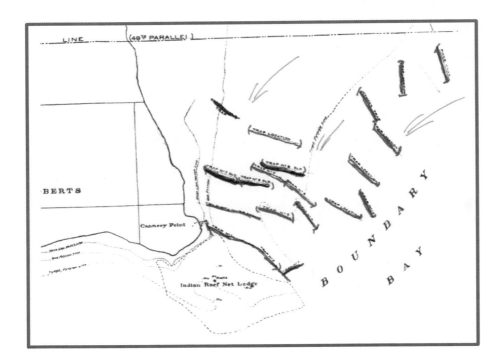

Fish Traps At Boundary Bay (Point Roberts) as mapped by Rathbun (Green shows traps, Red arrows delineates the route a major part of the sockeye run follows on its migration to the Fraser River)

Burgeoning demand for sockeye by Canadian canneries and, later, by canneries built at Point Roberts, on Lummi Island, and in other areas led to the near exclusion of tribal fishermen as an economic force and serious disruption in the cultural lives of those same fishermen and the families supported by them.

According to Rathbun in the mid-1890s, *"While we have little information on the subject, the traps as first constructed seem not to have been entirely suited to the capture of the sock eye, and the value of the different sites had yet to be learned. In Waller's trap the crib is said to have been only about 20 feet square while the leader, measuring some 900 feet long, did not approach nearer than 300 feet from, the shore. It was set only during the sockeye run, the greater portion of the catch being sold to the canneries on the Fraser River, while the remainder were salted."*

However, *"Mr. Waller was succeeded about 1885 by a practical fisherman from the Great Lakes, who is still at Point Roberts and who has done much to bring the net to its present state of perfection. He made use of at least the same general position as Mr. Waller, but in 1887 a second trap was added on the eastern side, much nearer the boundary line. Until 1891 the number of these nets does not seem to have been increased beyond two, the catch by this means continuing small and being disposed of as in the beginning."*

"In the last named year, however, a small cannery, the first one in the region, was built at Semiahmoo, at the eastern end of Boundary Bay, and arrangements were made to obtain the necessary supplies of fish from Point Roberts. This led to the erection of one or two, possibly three, additional traps. In 1893 a second cannery was built, this one occupying the southeast corner of the Point, and the number of traps was increased to 13, 11 being operated by the two canneries, and 2 independently. Before the next season both canneries had passed into the control of the Alaska Packers' Association, which made use of 12 traps during 1894, while 4 were under independent management, making 10 in all south of the boundary line."

"On the west side of Lummi Island, south of Village Point," Rathbun observed, *"Three trap-net sites, about equal distances apart, had been occupied up to the close of 1895...They lead off from the shore from 637 to 725 feet into depths of 6 to 8 fathoms."*

Fish traps threatened far more than a livelihood for the tribes of the Salish Straits; fish traps threatened to end a centuries old way of life. In response to the threat the Lummi asked for, and received, according to Rathbun, an injunction against the traps in 1895 but, after a long and convoluted court case, a case that went, on appeal, all the way to the Supreme Court of the United States. Inexplicably, the Bureau of Indian Affairs abandoned the case, at nearly the last moment, apparently without explanation, before the Court made the decision to accept or reject the case for argumentation.

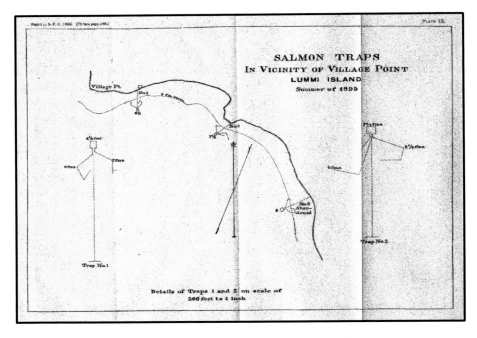

At Village Point on Lummi Island fish traps supported a major cannery but were
also a factor in devastating the reef net fishery

The result, as Rathbun reported was that, so far as the Indian
fishermen were concerned, *"In recent years their number has varied
from 150 to 200, though sometimes reaching 250. Their canoes have
been as many as 15 to 20, but lately the number has greatly fallen off
through the intervention of the whites. Their drying racks formerly
covered a considerable area, but they are now small in extent and
have been entirely driven from Cannery Point, their principal
location in more prosperous days. After the completion in 1894 of
the continuous line of traps commanding the approaches to the big
reef, its value for reef-net fishing seems to have been in great part
destroyed, and the Indian catches declined so much in consequence
as to render the old-time occupation practically unprofitable."*

By 1915, the days of the reef net fishery seemed to have ended. By
1921, John Cobb reported in the annual report of the U. S.
Commissioner of Fisheries that the reef net, *"At one time was a
favorite device of the Puget Sound natives for catching sockeye
salmon."* But, Cobb continued, *"Owing to the large number of men*

required to work them, and that fact that they can be worked only at certain stages of tide and in favorable weather, these nets gradually have been supplanted by other devices. In 1909 but five were used and these were operated off the shores of San Juan, Henry, Stewart, and Lummi Islands, and in the vicinity of Point Roberts. Practically none are used at present."

Salmon Trap photographed by John Cobb – 1921

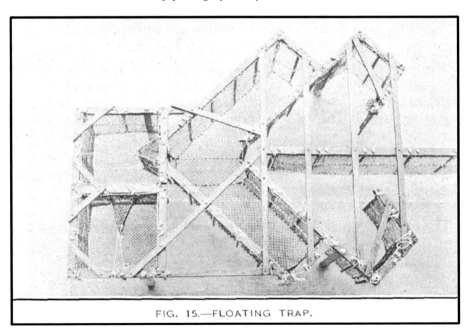

FIG. 15.—FLOATING TRAP.

1934: Fish Traps Outlawed And Reef Nets Begin A Comeback

Fisheries experts were warning about over-fishing and its consequences early in the 1880s, especially as it related to northern Puget Sound. A series of actions were taken to restrict the impact of fish traps and other devices but much damage had been done.

John Cobb, by 1921, had become one of the best known fisheries experts in the nation having helped found the University of Washington fisheries department (despite not possessing even a Bachelor's degree). Cobb addressed the issue in a report contained in the *Report of the United States Commissioner of the Fisheries* for 1921.

A huge slide had essentially blocked the Fraser River in 1913 and was being blamed for declines in the fish runs in Puget Sound. According to Cobb, *"That the subsequent decrease in the runs was not to be attributed solely to the rock slide in Hell Gate canyon is plainly evident by a glance at the (salmon) pack figures in this area and subsequent to 1913."*

Instead, Cobb put forward, *"Aside from the damage caused to the "big year" run by the rock slide, there can be only one explanation of such a progressive decline in the pack and that is excessive fishing."*

Cobb's placing of the blame on the fishing industry's shoulders is all the more remarkable in that while compiling a remarkable series of reports for the U.S. Commissioner of the Fisheries and while helping to found the University of Washington's fisheries department, he had also worked, until 1919, as the assistant superintendent of the Alaska Packers Association, one of largest canneries on the Sound.

Describing the gauntlet the Sockeye Salmon of the early 1900s had to run on the way to the spawning grounds of the Fraser, Cobb continued, *"The fishermen of both countries (Canada and the United States) are to blame for this. On the American side traps, purse seines, and, in a slight degree, gill nets have taken a heavy toll of the fish as they passed through our waters. After some had safely run this gantlet they met thousands of gill nets operated by Canadian fishermen in and around the mouth of the Fraser River and in the lower reaches of the same, and it is a wonder that any of the schools ever got to the spawning beds."*

REMOVING SALMON FROM TRAP NET OFF CANNERY POINT, POINT ROBERTS, WASHINGTON, 1895, TO SHOW HEAVY CONSTRUCTION OF THE CRIB IN THE LARGE TRAPS.

CANNERY POINT, POINT ROBERTS, WASHINGTON, 1895, SHOWING THE CANNERY ESTABLISHMENT AND THE STRING OF THREE TRAP NETS EXTENDING OFF FROM THE POINT.

Initiative 77, The Will Of The People

The Washington State Constitution contains the phrase, "The first power reserved by the people is the initiative." In 1934 the people of the state, fed up with the destruction of, particularly, the Sockeye salmon resource exercised the power reserved to them through the passage of "An Act relating to fishing; prohibiting the use of fish traps or other fixed appliances for catching salmon and certain other fish within the waters of the State of Washington; prohibiting the taking or fishing for salmon and certain other fish within a certain area therein defined and created by any means except by trolling, regulating trolling in such area, and permitting the operation of gill nets therein under certain conditions; providing for open and closed seasons, prohibiting drag seines and limiting the length of gill nets in the Columbia River; prescribing penalties; and repealing all laws in conflict therewith."

The initiative passed overwhelmingly with more than 64% of the turnout voting "yes."

Passage of the initiative marked the end of the age of the fish trap and, while it only put a dent in the pattern of resource abuse the traps were a symbol of, it did mark the beginning

Initiative Measure No. 77

BALLOT TITLE

An Act relating to fishing; prohibiting the use of fish traps or other fixed appliances for catching salmon and certain other fish within the waters of the State of Washington; prohibiting the taking or fishing for salmon and certain other fish within a certain area therein defined and created by any means except by trolling, regulating trolling in such area, and permitting the operation of gill nets therein under certain conditions; providing for open and closed seasons, prohibiting drag seines and limiting the length of gill nets in the Columbia River; prescribing penalties; and repealing all laws in conflict therewith.

An Act relating to the taking and catching of fish; prescribing a district within the State of Washington in the waters of which it is made unlawful to take, catch, or fish for any salmon, by any means except by the use of hook and line, setting forth the boundaries of said district, and for licensing the operation, and for the operation of gill nets by certain persons, firms and corporations holding licenses for the use of such gill nets in 1932 or 1933; providing for com- nected therewith within the State of Washington described as lying to the Southerly, Easterly and Southeasterly of a line described as follows:

Commencing at a concrete monument on Angeles Point in Clallam County, State of Washington, near the mouth of the Elwha River, on which is inscribed "Angeles Point Monument" in latitude 48° 9' 3" North, longitude 123° 23' 61" West of Greenwich Meridian; thence running East on a line 81° 39' true from said point across the Flashlight and bell buoy off Partridge

of a much greater public awareness in the public mind of the importance the fisheries resource represented to not only Washington's economy but its obligation to act as stewards of the environment. It also provided for a resurgence in the reef net industry; a return to a kinder and gentler approach to resource use.

Beatrice Annette Lowman was the daughter of a Puget Sound cannery owner who, in the post Initiative 77 world became one of the nation's most famous salmon fishers. Needing money to pay off college debt (Beatrice was a graduate of the University of Washington), Beatrice wrangled a job on a reef net boat in 1938 and became an overnight sensation after introducing herself as "Reef Net Betty" in a magazine article. *"Dear Puget Sounder,"* Betty wrote, *"Here goes with the letter you asked for about the only girl fisherman in the United Fishermen's Union of the Pacific – just husky freckled me – Reef Net Betty of the Puget Sound Islands."*

Betty was already a well-known adventurer when she took up reef net fishing having gained local fame at fourteen as the youngest person ever (at the time at least) to swim the frigid, mile wide, Guemes Channel between Anacortes and Guemes Island in Puget Sound. On graduating from university Betty fitted out an old Indian canoe to accommodate oars and set out to row solo the 1,300 miles between the Sound and Ketchikan, Alaska, a sixty-six day trip highlighted by a capsizing and the spending of three days stranded before being rescued by Indian fishermen.

Betty was bigger than life. She was outgoing, adventurous, bold, broke, and in most ways, save for being nearly the lone female in the reef net fraternity, completely typical of the new breed of reef netters entering the fishery in the wake of Initiative 77; the Great Depression was nearing an end but still raging and people were desperate to make a living. The reef net seemed to offer the potential to make that living.

Aside from an unquenchable exuberance, Betty has something few others could offer; a degree in journalism from the University of Washington. Betty was an accomplished writer; her writings provide one of the clearest pictures available today of the growth of the reef net fishery immediately after the passing of the fish traps.

A Chronical Of Hard Times

Economic hope was on the horizon and Initiative 77 had been passed. As told by Betty, the impact of the initiative had been two-fold. *"The reef net which is said to mark the acme of Indian invention flourished until the white man (my pioneer salmon canneryman grandfather among them) brought in fish traps. For a long time then, reef nets were unprofitable and almost entirely disappeared. Then Initiative 77 resulted in the abolishment of traps, a crash in our family finances, the return of reef nets, and in my fishing on one of the bally things with a crew of three men – all big, strong, ex-loggers and strangers at first."*

Along with everyone else in the day, Betty needed work. She found it as a flood of eager entrepreneurs saw the potential in the old way of fishing, a technology requiring little investment but a lot of hard work.

A Rush To Reef Net

As Betty described it, Initiative 77 had passed as the result of two interest groups working in concert to convince voters to vote "Yes" on the ballot measure; purse seine fishermen and sports fishing advocates had worked together to promote the idea that eliminating fish traps was important to the conservation of the resource. According to Betty, purse seiners were *"triumphant"* at the passage.

By 1939 Betty wrote, in an article for *Pacific Fisherman* magazine, *"...their joy is slightly squelched. Where fish traps once helped the purse seiner by schooling and detaining fish along wire netting leads, there are now, in the same American fishing areas, dozens of cluttering reef net gears. These are an ancient Indian invention for catching sockeye salmon, and are no help to the purse seine fisherman.*

Reef Net fishermen in Legoe Bay, Lummi Island: *Pacific Fisherman* – 1939

According to Betty no more than nine reef nets had fished the waters of Puget Sound in the years 1909 to 1932 but, on adoption of Initiative 77, a "pink gold rush" took place. *"In 1934 there were ten licenses issued for reef nets. In 1935 twice that many owners were experimenting with the Indian idea, and in 1936, the second year after the abolishment of fish traps there were 32 reef nets in Puget Sound, the only fishing ground in the world where they are used. In 1937 there were 49 such rigs, slightly improved, and last summer the number jumped to 74, with more white men than Indians using this type of gear, and cannerymen becoming definitely interested."*

Open Warfare: Purse Seiners vs Reef Net Fishermen

The euphoria felt by the purse seiners over the defeat of the fish trap owners in 1934 soon turned to antagonism. The use of the very simple gear formerly used by the Indians of the Sound led to the seiners viewing reef netters, especially white reef net fishermen, as being "usurpers," unfairly taking advantage of  an Indian technology on fishing grounds the seiners considered to be proprietary. No matter the seiners had done the same to the fish trap owners utilizing the right to initiative enshrined in the Washington State Constitution.

The result was near warfare between the two groups. As described by Betty, *"With the increase in gear, considerable friction arose between purse seiners and reef netters. Seiners with their power boats frequently spread their nets in front of reef net rigs, threatening to ruin them; and once in 1937, angry Legoe Bay reef*

*netters slashed an offending seine to pieces. They were hailed (*sic)
*into court but nothing has come of it. Reef netters at Lopez have
stood off purse seiners by taking pot shots at them with a rifle.*"

New Technologies And New Opportunities

Post Initiative 77. fishermen and women were both adopting and
adapting the reef net approaches invented by the Straits Salish of
pre-contact times.

Even before the era of the fish traps, when the Straits Salish were
almost alone in using reef nets, cordage was having an impact on the
fishery. Stronger nets and stronger, and longer, anchor lines were
allowing fishing in deeper water and presumably, less escapement
due to breakage; but old car frames filled with boulders? That's a
technology Betty pointed to that had to wait until 1934!

Like the Coast Salish, the reef net fisherman of the 1930s used two
boats. According to Betty, "*Although Indians used dugout canoes,
the white man has built flat-bottomed, double-ended boats from 25
to 40 ft. long. A few of the latest models have square sterns, and
decking of numbers boards to form the fish bins.*"

The Layout Of The Gear

"*Each gear,*" Betty reported, "*Has four anchors, one inshore from
the inside boat and one outside the outer boat, and one 100 to 200 ft.
from the bow of each boat. Log buoys mark the head anchor cables
and also the far end of each buoy line, which leads to the bow of its
corresponding boat; the two forming a funnel on the surface of the
water. This "funnel" is marked by three foot wooden buoys, some
crude and some carefully whittled. These buoy lines converge from
the approximately 200 ft. gap at the head buoys to the two open
boats between which the net is spread. Boats and net are
comparable to the tube of the funnel, a tube that averages 40 feet in
width.*"

"*Two ropes fastened from 25 to 35 ft. down the head anchor cables
slant upward to the front of the weighted net.*" Betty continued.

"These are the 'net lines.' From each buoy line to the net line under it are tied six-thread 'sidelines' at intervals of about a fathom.

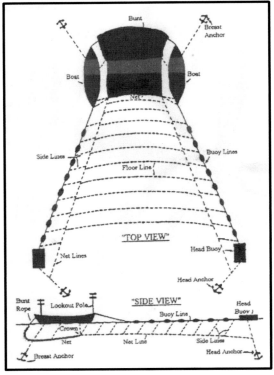

Across the funnel from net line to net line are spread from ten to thirty 'floorlines' at the same intervals. Every three feet or so in the ply of sidelines and floorlines the crew inserts stalks of silvery marsh grass (replaced anew every few weeks), and so they create the appearance of a reef.

Under this imitation "reef" may be as much as 15 fathoms of water: but the salmon tend to swim above it, and to keep in mid-channel between the sidelines, although these lines and grass stalks present no real obstruction.

Most successful gears are those on which the sidelines arch upward from the head anchors and down again to the net. The theory is that salmon swim to the top of the arch, see the dark net as a deep hole on the far side of the "reef" and swim down rapidly within the range of vision of fishermen watching through their polaroid sun glasses."

Bringing In The Fish

Describing how the fish are caught, Betty put forward, *"On the bow of each boat are look-out poles or stands on which fishermen cling through storms and good weather for flash, fin, bubble, or quiver of salmon. Others in the crew sit quietly, fearful of frightening the fish more than they are already frightened by being pursued by seine* boats all the way in from the ocean. The customary shout at sight of fish in the net is, "Give 'em Hell!" and the motionless crew snaps into action.

The strip of dark net suspended between the boats is commonly 42 by 48 ft. of 3 ¼ in. mesh. At the forward corners of the net, sunk to 20 ft. or more by heavy lead sinkers, are block lines by which the rib-lined front of the net is hand-lifted. Bunt lines at the back corners restrain the net as the tide running against it causes it to bag or purse where the web is gathered to the bunt line. Middle lines also help in hauling the net and pocketing the salmon.

With fish definitely confined, breast anchor lines are slacked off and the boats move together as fishermen pull against each other at the net. As quickly as the salmon, untouched by any...are dumped into one of the boats, the net is loosened and lowered and the boats are pulled back to their original position."

As a good journalist should, Betty also paid attention to the innovations the flood of eager new reef netters were trying out. The new-fangled polarized sunglasses invented by Edwin Land (inventor of the Polaroid Land Camera) were brought to market in 1937, just in time to optimize results from another innovation to the reef net boat, the watch or lookout tower most boats sported in Betty's day. Better cordage meant winches could be used to replace some jobs formerly done by hand. At Point Roberts and at Legoe Bay double-ended pontoon boats were introduced to replace one of the open boats previously used allowing for fishing to continue even in times of rough water that would have made ordinary fishing too hazardous to continue.

Winches were utilized in an on-going series of experiments, according to Betty with the result that fishermen were able to adjust their rigs to the vagaries of tide and current rather than be restricted to fishing only at times when the current was ideal.

Clouds On The Horizon

War between the reef netters and the purse seiners over the right to fish began almost before the votes on Initiative 77 were counted. In addition to physical violence and harassment, seiners began a years long effort to make reef netting illegal in Washington waters.

Reef Net Betty addressed the issues in her article for *Pacific Fishing*, laying out not only the legal grounds the seiners intended to rely on but a rebuttal as well. *"Greatest psychological arguments used in 1934 to abolish traps were that ownership was monopolized by certain capitalistic interests, and that traps hindered conservation by blocking escapement to spawning streams;"* Betty wrote. *"But old stories of monopoly dangers to conservation, and the "fixed appliance" prohibition of "Initiative 77" do not apply to this method of fishing,* (reef netting) *which is described by the earliest navigators to visit the Pacific Northwest."*

Also, Betty contended, since reef net licenses given by the state did not designate specific sites, and because reef net boats and their gear could be towed from site to site, the reef net fishery could not be considered to be regulated by the Initiative prohibition.

The 1940s – Regulation, Growth, And Unity

By the time the opportunities offered by Initiative 77 began to be fully felt, America was coming out of the Great Depression but was only a year or two away from World War. The State began to increase its regulatory efforts, the reef netters come together to form Local 4 of the Puget Sound Reefnetters Union, and the industry began to stabilize after the rapid growth of 1937 through '39. By 1950 "no salmon fishing" preserves had been established based on Initiative 77 and various areas had been marked off and were regulated "…according to the type of gear utilized." An uneasy peace existed between the seiners and the reef netters, undoubtedly brought about by the fact that the nation was at war. All was soon to change.

Seiners had been irritated from the start about reef nets, charging reef nets were "fixed appliances" and, as such, had been outlawed by the Initiative.

Everything came to a head in 1954 as a legal challenge to reef netting came before the Washington State Supreme Court and, in coordination with the challenge, an Initiative to the people that would, among other things, ban the use of reef nets was brought to the ballot.

Reef netters fought back. The Washington Reef Net Owners Association and the Puget Sound Reef Netters Union, Local 44 combined to hire Bellingham attorney David Rhea to intervene in the case, a case brought forward by one Mike Pirak the owner of a fishing boat plying the waters of Puget Sound.

The Setting For The Case Against Reef Netting

The end of World War Two had brought a resurgence in the reef net industry. According to the suit Pirak and his fellows alleged, before the court, "…that five years ago there were only forty licenses issued for reef nets, but the number has steadily increased, and in 1953 one hundred forty licenses were issued." The petitioners alleged that not only was the State's director of fisheries intending to renew existing license, he was willing to *"...issue new licenses for reef nets for the year 1954."*

According to Pirak reef nets were, *"...a boxlike device which is enclosed on three sides and the bottom, and open on one side for the entry of salmon. It is made stationary in the water by the use of anchors and other means, and remains in one location for the entire fishing season."*

As described by the Supreme Court, "This proceeding was instituted to prohibit the state director of fisheries from issuing licenses for the use of reef nets in the catching of salmon."

Even as the legal challenge played out an Initiative To The People was placed on the ballot for 1954. The Initiative added reef nets to the various fishing methods already banned nearly two decades previously.

Lake Washington preserve includes those waters within a radius of three miles from the west entrance to Ballard Locks;

Duwamish preserve includes Elliott Bay east of a line drawn from Four Mile rock to Alki Point light;

Snohomish preserve includes all waters of Port Gardner inside lines Range 3 and 4 east Snohomish County, Washington.

SECTION 3. It shall be unlawful to construct, install, use, operate or maintain, within any of the waters of the state of Washington, any pound net, fish trap, fish wheel, scow fish wheel, set net, reef net, round haul net, lampara net, or any fixed appli-

[14]

Initiative Measure No. 192 (Continued)

ance for the purpose of catching salmon.

in violation of this Act, and the articles seized shall be confiscated to the state regardless of the ownership

Initiative Measure 192 sought to eliminate reef nets from Puget Sound

Faced with a fight for existence, reef net supporters went to work, providing newspaper editors with information, producing flyers and handouts, and personally working to influence the vote on the initiative arguing the initiative was nothing more than an attempt to monopolize the fisheries by "the big boys," by putting small scale fishermen like the reef netters out of business. Worse, according to the reef netters, the mobile, commercial fishermen wanted to expand their fishery into areas set aside as conservation preserves and thus, jeopardize the future of the fishery for both commercial and sports fishermen; "scientific" control of the fisheries of the sound by the Department of Fisheries would be replaced by a regulatory scheme focused on providing financial benefit to those responsible for bringing the initiative to the ballot in the first place.

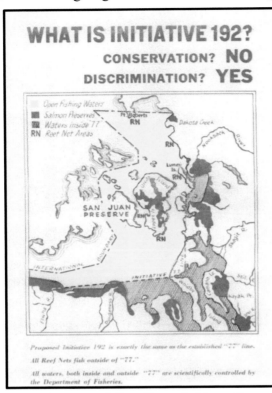

WHAT IS INITIATIVE 192?
CONSERVATION? **NO**
DISCRIMINATION? **YES**

Open Fishing Waters
■ *Salmon Preserves*
▨ *Waters inside 77*
RN *Reef Net Areas*

Proposed Initiative 192 is exactly the same as the established "77" line.
All Reef Nets fish outside of "77."
All waters, both inside and outside "77" are scientifically controlled by the Department of Fisheries.

The Purpose Of An Attack On Two Fronts

The attack on reef netters seems to have been carefully planned. If the seine fishermen won in court, reef nets would be considered a variety of "fish trap" and found to be illegal. A win in court would have made the Initiative 192 moot so far as reef nets were concerned; the reef netters would have lost their livelihood no matter the result of the public vote.

A loss in court would have been overruled by a win at the ballot box because the new Initiative would have superseded Initiative 77 by specifying reef nets as a prohibited technique for the salmon fishery.

Only a win in court *and* a win at the ballot box could save the industry.

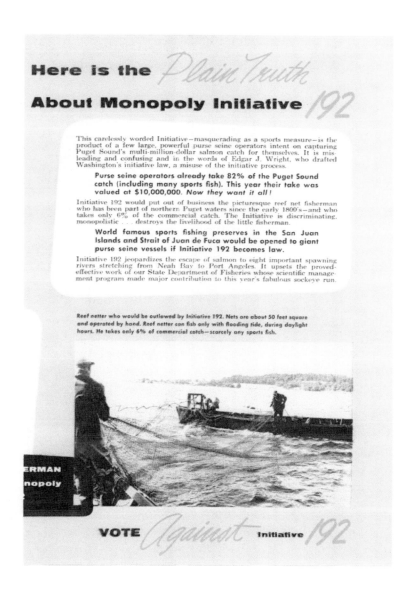

Here is the *Plain Truth*

About Monopoly Initiative *192*

This carelessly worded Initiative—masquerading as a sports measure—is the product of a few large, powerful purse seine operators intent on capturing Puget Sound's multi-million-dollar salmon catch for themselves. It is misleading and confusing and in the words of Edgar J. Wright, who drafted Washington's initiative law, a misuse of the initiative process.

Purse seine operators already take 82% of the Puget Sound catch (including many sports fish). This year their take was valued at $10,000,000. Now they want it all!

Initiative 192 would put out of business the picturesque reef net fisherman who has been part of northern Puget waters since the early 1800's—and who takes only 6% of the commercial catch. The Initiative is discriminating, monopolistic . . . destroys the livelihood of the little fisherman.

World famous sports fishing preserves in the San Juan Islands and Strait of Juan de Fuca would be opened to giant purse seine vessels if Initiative 192 becomes law.

Initiative 192 jeopardizes the escape of salmon to eight important spawning rivers stretching from Neah Bay to Port Angeles. It upsets the proved-effective work of our State Department of Fisheries whose scientific management program made major contribution to this year's fabulous sockeye run.

Reef netter who would be outlawed by Initiative 192. Nets are about 50 feet square and operated by hand. Reef netter can fish only with flooding tide, during daylight hours. He takes only 6% of commercial catch—scarcely any sports fish.

ERMAN
nopoly

VOTE *Against* **Initiative** *192*

The High Tide Of Modern Reef Netting

November 1954 cannot have been a happy time for the seiners and their associates. November 2nd the people listened to the entreaties of the reef netters and rejected Initiative 192 by a resounding margin.

Now the seiner's hopes rested solely on the pending decision from the Washington State Supreme Court. November 18 the Court issued its opinion, reef nets were not stationary, not prohibited.

While the reef net community celebrated its victory, all was not everything everyone would wish. In January of 1954 the Department of Fisheries had made it clear, in a letter regarding an appeal to reverse the rejection of a reef net set at Lummi Island that regulation would be on-going and not always to the liking of either the reef net owners or the reef net union.

In justifying its decision the department wrote, *"The reef netting operations on Puget Sound reached the height of expansion in 1949 and the rapid spread of gear obviously was leading to court litigation because of interference with other established gear with a long tradition of free use of the waters in certain areas.*

Since that time the Department has attempted to exercise a reasonable control of the reef net fishery, and to cut back as many as possible of the conflicting locations. We believe that with one or two exceptions the fishery is now in as good balance relative to other gear as can be accomplished without undue hardship."

In short, the Department was not about to take "sides" in disputes between seiners, reef netters, and sports fishers. The Department would retain firm control and management of the entire fishery.

1934 – 1970

A Master Reef Netter's Perspective

1970 was a year of stress for the fishing industry. Regulators, tribes, sports fishers, and commercial fishers alike were faced with uncertainty as all pondered an uncertain future once the Federal Courts made what eventually came to be called the "Boldt Decision."

Warren Granger of Lummi Island, one of the most respected of the region's reef net fishermen wrote about the industry he'd participated in for more than three decades, especially while fishing the waters of Legoe Bay off Village Point. Warren wrote, in part:

In the interest of possibly shedding some additional light on the present controversy (the Federal Case before Judge Boldt), *involving the legitimacy of the Reef-Net Gear fishery, I have decided to record some of my recollections and thoughts*  *regarding this type of fishery in general and that located in Legoe Bay in particular.*

Being a native of Lummi Island since 1903, and personally engaged in the Reef-Net gear fishery since 1938, I have more than a casual acquaintance with the development of this part of the fishing industry. During the years of my earliest recollections the fish traps were dominant and they had acquired a virtual monopoly. They were "Big Business," expensive to install and maintain, and were located, within legal limits, any place where the contour of the shore, set of the currents, depth of water and nature of the bottom permitted piling to be driven, and fish to swim close inshore. These devices were highly efficient and soon eliminated the primitive types of Indian fishing.

By 1913...the increasing number and efficiency of purse seines was giving the traps plenty of competition. The salmon runs rapidly declined under the joint onslaught of these two methods, together with the diminished access to the spawning grounds.

Finally, as an act of desperation, to prevent the total extinction of the resource the State of Washington by initiative vote outlawed fish traps completely. Among other things this action clearly established the State's legal right to regulate any and all fishing within its waters. So, following this action of the voters in 1936, opportunity was provided for establishing small, inshore, owner-operated fisheries in the most likely locations."

"One such spot," Warren continued, *"Was Legoe Bay along the south west shore of Lummi Island.*

In 1937 three or four enterprising individuals located a like number of Reef-net Type Gears near the area vacated by the old Alsop Trap. *In 1938 another eight or ten gears were established including my own. Also, the area was extended along the shore both ways, toward Village Point and eastward off the Bluff.*

All of these rigs represented considerable individual effort. Operators build their own boats, anchors, buoys, winches, etc. This process continued to expand over the next few years until at the peak, more than fifty gears were located in the area, which extended all of the way from Village Point to Lummi Rocks.

Along with building and improving our equipment and techniques we had to develop our own local regulations, shore installations, and water borne means of handling heavy anchors... ten or fifteen tons weight.

In 1954 arose a crisis wherein we were forced to fight for our existence against Initiative 192 by means of which our competitors hoped to eliminate us from the industry. This was a difficult and expensive battle in which the voters gave us a three to one victory."

Despite The Win The Fishery Declines

Warren describes the 1960s as a time of continuing stress for the Reef Net fishery as regulation and increased competition takes a toll on small business operators. *"Throughout the 1960's it became necessary to protect the salmon fishery by the most stringent regulations, - curtailing fishing time to one or two days per week, early and late closures, and some times, complete shutdowns. Many times just when it seemed we were going to make out all right for the season the fishery would be closed in order to assure sufficient spawners to escape to the spawning grounds to reproduce the various races of salmon. This made operating at a profit*

exceedingly hazardous and the number of Reef-net Type Gears steadily declined until today less than half the 1954 number remain.

"Coincidently," Warren adds, apparently with tongue firmly in cheek, *"The numbers of gill and purse seine nets tripled during this period. The "survivor," to stay in business had to streamline their operations, i.e., more durable materials, better maintenance, and in some cases a reduction in crew members."*

Speaking to some of the issues in the Federal Case before the Court even as he wrote, Warren contended, *"Certainly, the present operation bears slight resemblance to the primitive Indian fishery. Actually, it's not even done in the same place. The original Indian fishery was close inshore. Cedar bark ropes and nets, rock anchors and dugout canoes could never be operated in the present locations. In fact, the places fished by the Indians 100 years ago are still vacant. The vast salmon runs of those days could be fished by practically "sitting on the beach."*

2018 – An Industry Reinvents Itself

Today, the modern reef net fishing industry has, in some sense, come full circle; only a handful of boats ply the waters of Lummi Island's Legoe Bay, scarcely more than fished immediately after Initiative 77 ended the era of the fish trap; But many believe a new era of entrepreneurial environmentalism is leading to a resurgence of the industry.

Washington State's Department of Fish and Wildlife identifies the use of selective commercial fishing gear as an idea to be pursued and says, "Reef nets stand out as the original and still the best in selective fishing."

What does that all mean? Forward thinking grocers are featuring reef net caught products as not only tasting better (the fish aren't killed and then left on ice for some unspecified period of time before either sale or processing takes place) but as being good for the environment because, unlike nearly every other technology utilized for catching fish, reef netting does not result in the killing of "by catch" or fish caught accidentally. Fish caught using a reef net are placed into a bin and stay alive until removed from the boat. Unwanted fish, caught up in the net meant for target fish are taken out of the net when it is pulled to the surface and tossed back into the sea. Studies have shown almost no death of by catch occurs when reef nets are utilized while most other methods of catching fish results in the death of unwanted species.

The indigenous peoples of the Salish Sea, hundreds of years ago, understood the value of maintaining the environment fish needed to continue the life cycle of the species into the future. The tribes of today understand as well, the need to care for the environment they, and the fish they value require to survive into the future.

Completing the circle? In recent years the original people of the reef net are rediscovering the technology they invented so many centuries ago and are once again fishing the seas they once commanded.

The future of reef netting rests on the same foundation it has rested on since the first indigenous genius figured out how to use the combination of reef, ocean currents, fish biology, and simple gear to serve the needs of the people; respect for the environment; respect for all people; and respect for the greatest fish of all – the Sockeye Salmon!

Lummi Fishermen Pursue The Sockeye Salmon In The 1930s

The Salish Sea

Below is a map of the Salish Sea and its surrounding basin produced in 2009 by Stefan Freelan, a WWU cartographer. Freelan explains:

The SALISH SEA (formally designated in 2009) *extends from the north end of the Strait of Georgia and Desolation Sound to the south end of the Puget Sound and west to the mouth of the Strait of Juan de Fuca, including the inland marine waters of southern British Columbia, Canada and northern Washington, USA.*

Acknowledgements

Jeff Jewell of the Whatcom Museum is aptly named. He is a Whatcom County treasure. The authors thank Jeff for his help and the Whatcom County Museum for the use of some of the treasures contained in the Museum's photo archives.

Some confusion exists regarding the designation, in 2009/10 of a new name for the marine inland waters of both Washington State and British Columbia by both Canada and the United States. Stefan Freelan's map of the newly named "Salish Sea," along with conversation accompanying the map should clear up any confusion. Find excellent PDFs of the map and additional information at: http://staff.wwu.edu/stefan/salish_sea.shtml. Thank you Stefan

Thanks to the University of Washington Special Collections library for two images.

The color image of a male sockeye salmon is from Timothy Knepp of the Fish and Wildlife Service. - US Fish and Wildlife Service

The men and women of past centuries who made it their life's work to study the lives and cultures of the indigenous peoples of North America's west coast for having left behind an invaluable record that should be passed on before it is forgotten and lost in the *myths* of time.